Original title:
Sowing Sonnets

Copyright © 2025 Creative Arts Management OÜ
All rights reserved.

Author: Levi Montgomery
ISBN HARDBACK: 978-1-80566-624-0
ISBN PAPERBACK: 978-1-80566-909-8

The Poetry of Growth

In the garden, seeds take flight,
They dance and twirl, oh what a sight!
With watering cans, we sing our songs,
Each sprout a joke that can't be wrong.

The tomatoes blush, the peppers giggle,
As carrots tease with each little wiggle.
The radishes play hide and seek,
Beneath the soil, they peek-a-boo sneak!

Garden of Whispers

In the beds where laughter grows,
The daisies chat with the garden hose.
They gossip sweetly about the sun,
And giggle softly, oh isn't it fun?

The mushrooms murmur in evening light,
Sharing secrets without a fright.
A beet laughs out, 'I'm sweet, not shy!'
While butterflies flutter and pass on by.

Nature's Hidden Lyrics

The bees are buzzing a tune so bright,
In harmony with the stars at night.
Each flower hums a little rhyme,
In the grassy fields, it's party time!

The crickets chirp, a rhythmic beat,
As frogs croak out their crooning feat.
Nature's band in a joyful spree,
Twirling under the old oak tree.

Cultivated Expressions

In the patch where veggies wear their hats,
Cucumbers chat with the playful rats.
With lettuce giggles and overgrown peas,
They debate the best way to catch the breeze.

The herbs conspire with scents so bold,
Telling tales that never grow old.
Each vine a story, each leaf a jest,
In this garden party, we're all impressed!

Melodies of the Meadow

In the meadow, bees do dance,
Chasing flowers in a trance.
Butterflies wear their silly hats,
While rabbits sing to chubby cats.

Grasshoppers jump with a cheeky grin,
Trying hard to fit right in.
A snail slips on a leafy slide,
While daisies giggle, side by side.

Gentle Echoes of Imagination

In the forest, squirrels scheme,
Wishing on a fluffy dream.
They build castles in the air,
With acorns stashed beyond compare.

A clever fox plays hide and seek,
In the shadows, oh so sleek.
The trees chuckle, leaves will sway,
As creatures laugh the day away.

The Language of Blooms

Tulips chatter, roses tease,
They whisper secrets with the breeze.
Daisies tell a zany tale,
Of a snail who rode a whale!

Sunflowers wave their golden heads,
Dreaming of dancing on their beds.
Pansies giggle, what a sight,
As colors clash in pure delight.

Tender Lines of Growth

In a garden, veggies grin,
Carrots cheer for the first spin.
Lettuce laughs, with leafy flair,
While peas debate who's most rare.

Tomatoes squabble, redder than sin,
While radishes show off their skin.
Together, they sway in the sun's bright glow,
A comedy act, putting on a show.

Cultures of the Heart

In the garden of my chest, I grow,
With humor blooms, a lively show.
Each chuckle sprout, a giggle leaf,
Transforming woes into comic relief.

Watered with puns, sunlit with cheer,
They flourish bright, drawing laughter near.
A heart that's light, a jester's art,
Tending the joy, in cultures of the heart.

Tending the Literary Orchard

In my orchard of words, I plant the seeds,
Nurtured with laughter, they sprout like weeds.
Rhymes twist and twirl, like vines intertwined,
Creating a harvest that's whimsically aligned.

With rhyme as the shovel and puns as the rake,
I prune silly lines for the giggles' sake.
A crop of delight from my whimsical mind,
In my literary orchard, hilarity's kind.

Whispers of the Seed

Tiny whispers drift on the breeze,
Seeds of laughter dance with such ease.
From the tiniest joke to the wildest jest,
In the soil of humor, they flourish best.

Grow and giggle, watch them entwine,
Sprouting smiles that twist and twine.
Each laugh a petal, bright and free,
Whispers of joy from the roots of glee.

Verses in the Wind

Verses flutter like kites in the air,
Floating on laughter, with nary a care.
In the breeze they twirl, a whimsical spin,
Each line a giggle, every word a grin.

Carry my sonnets where the chuckles dwell,
Tickling the clouds, casting humor's spell.
As the wind sings sweet, a perky hymn,
Verses take flight, on laughter's whim.

Harvesting Inspiration

In rows of laughter, seeds we throw,
A twist of words, the best we know.
With each small sprout, a chuckle grows,
In every rhyme, a humor flows.

The sun smiles bright on silly dreams,
As we pick thoughts from bubbling streams.
Chasing shadows and brightening days,
In every line, a playful praise.

Gathering joy in baskets wide,
With puns and giggles as our guide.
We dance in fields of clever wit,
Harvesting humor, bit by bit.

So come and join this merry plot,
Where planting words is all we've got.
With laughter's fruit, the best to share,
A garden filled with love and care.

Verses from the Garden

Digging deep where humor hides,
We plant our lines like wily guides.
In every corner, jokes unfold,
A patch of giggles, bright and bold.

Tending blooms of playful phrasing,
Nurtured by our silly gazing.
We prune the weeds of serious tone,
And let the laughter happily roam.

With watering cans of puns in hand,
We cultivate a joyous land.
Each line a rose, each word a petal,
In our funny garden, we are settled.

So let's rejoice in our backyard,
Where wit and whimsy find reward.
With every harvest, cheer will gleam,
In verses sprouted from a dream.

Nature's Gentle Lines

In fields of rhyme where daisies dance,
We plant our phrases, take a chance.
With clouds of laughter drifting by,
We sketch the skies and wonder why.

The breeze gives voice to jokes in flight,
While crickets chirp their laughs at night.
With gentle strokes, the sun will tease,
Creating art among the trees.

Every leaf a chance to play,
In nature's brush, we find our way.
So grab a plant and join this fun,
As lines take root beneath the sun.

With whimsical flair in every breeze,
We share our joy with buzzing bees.
Nature smiles as we craft our lines,
In a world full of witty signs.

Gardener of Words

With shovel, spade, and hat askew,
I dig for lines, a jester's view.
In earth's embrace, I plant with cheer,
A garden where good humor's near.

Each seed a pun that winks and grins,
A harvest full of giggle wins.
Tending phrases, bright and spry,
In the orchard of the witty sky.

Snipping words and watering dreams,
Cultivating joyful schemes.
With a laugh, I trim the vines,
To share the fruit of silly lines.

So join me in this quirky plot,
Where every jest is often sought.
In the garden of our quirky play,
Let's weave some joy into the day.

Harvesting Elegy

In fields of laughter, corn grows tall,
A scarecrow jokes, he's having a ball.
The pumpkins giggle, tricks on their vines,
While raccoons dance in moonlit signs.

With every plow, a pun is found,
As carrots wiggle and dance around.
The turnips titter in the breeze,
While beans share jokes with the swaying trees.

Blooming with Words

A garden of puns blooms in the sun,
Where daisies debate who's the funniest one.
The roses recite their latest quips,
While tulips engage in comic flips.

With laughter echoing on scented trails,
The violets whisper their whimsical tales.
In this patch of chuckles, humor takes flight,
As bees buzz by, feeling delight.

Seasons of the Soul

In spring, we laugh at the rain's thick plot,
While cheerful raindrops dance on the spot.
Summer brings burns, oh what a scene,
As sun hats tip over, quite comically keen.

Autumn arrives with leaves that delight,
They tumble and giggle, a colorful sight.
And winter, oh winter, brings snowball fights,
As snowmen crack jokes beneath starry nights.

Fertile Grounds of Thought

Intellect grows in quirky patches,
Where ideas sprout and laughter catches.
The seedlings chuckle, rooting with glee,
While thoughts blossom like a wild jubilee.

With every question, a joke takes flight,
In this fertile ground, things feel so right.
So plant those seeds of wit with care,
And watch as humor blooms everywhere!

Chasing the Sunlit Muse

In the chase of light we run,
With giggles bright like morning sun.
For thoughts that flit like butterflies,
Are caught with laughter, not with sighs.

We skip and twirl on grassy hills,
Where joy, like sugar, sweetly spills.
Each quirky thought a playful tease,
A dance with scribbles in the breeze.

Petals of Memory

Memories flutter like soft leaves,
Tickling toes and even sleeves.
Each one a story, wrapped in cheer,
With goofy grins and moments dear.

We pluck the blooms of yesteryear,
And laugh at how we shed a tear.
For every petal bears a jest,
In the quilt of laughs we all invest.

Imagery in Full Bloom

Imagination blooms like a rose,
The wilder the thought, the greater it grows.
With colors bright and shapes that spin,
Each quirky twist is where we begin.

The canvas splotched in paint and fun,
A masterpiece 'neath a laughing sun.
With every splash and silly stroke,
We plant our dreams and dance, provoke.

The Rhythm of the Earth

The earth hums tunes beneath our feet,
With wobbly beats that make us greet.
We jig and jive to nature's flow,
As silly thoughts begin to grow.

From creaky trees to buzzing bees,
The world's a stage, it aims to please.
So let's twirl in the soil's embrace,
And play our laughter in this space.

The Canvas of Nature

In fields where crayons dance and twirl,
The daisies wear their painted pearls.
A butterfly dons a polka-dot tie,
While grass sings songs as bees buzz by.

The trees are artists with leafy hands,
Creating shadows across the lands.
A squirrel poses, cheeky and bold,
Holding an acorn like it's pure gold.

The clouds play tags in the azure sky,
As rain drops laugh, then slip and slide.
A garden gnome rolls in the sun,
Declaring that work is not much fun.

So let's grab brushes, and join this spree,
In nature's palette, wild and free.
We'll paint our dreams with a joyous brush,
And giggle as we feel that playful rush.

Vibrant Poetry

When words jump out like froggy leaps,
They wiggle and giggle in policies of peeps.
Each stanza wears a silly hat,
While rhymes get tangled like an old house cat.

The verses hum a jolly tune,
Dancing beneath the teasing moon.
In gardens where the tomatoes quarrel,
I find my muse wrapped up in a brawl.

Chasing commas with a bouncy ball,
Words tumble and fumble, oh what a sprawl!
With metaphors like spaghetti strands,
I write myself into whimsical lands.

So just grab a pen and let thoughts bloom,
Let laughter echo through every room.
In vibrant colors, we'll craft our speech,
With a sprinkle of fun, and a lesson to teach.

Rhythmic Roots

The roots below do twist and twine,
In a dance that's mostly benign.
While worms wiggle in a friendly race,
And the mud wears a mischievous face.

Beetles drum on hollow logs,
While frogs croak out the latest vogues.
Each heartbeat in the soil we feel,
Like nature's very own big wheel.

And as the sun rolls through the trees,
The whispers tickle like a summer breeze.
With every bound and every jump,
Life's rhythmic roots give quite the thump!

So let us play the forest's song,
In this silly dance where we belong.
With laughter echoing through the glades,
We'll celebrate all the quirky shades.

Blossoming in Silence

In quiet gardens where giggles bloom,
The flowers nod, dispelling gloom.
Petals whisper secrets sweet and small,
While butterflies hold a silent ball.

Amidst the greens, a grumpy snail,
Sips dew from leaves while telling a tale.
In shimmery teacups, raindrops sing,
As daisies don their wedding ring.

With sun-kissed smiles, the tulips sway,
Winking at clouds that drift away.
And in this quietness, we find our cheer,
As nature laughs, and we all hear.

So join this dance of blooming things,
Where silence carries the joy it brings.
In petaled whispers, there's room to roam,
Creating laughter in our green home.

Blossoming Ideas

In the garden of thoughts, I plant my seeds,
Watering dreams like they're tiny weeds.
Fertilizer giggles, sunbeams have fun,
Hoping my mind's produce weighs a ton.

Worms in the soil, they wriggle and dance,
Competing with flowers for the best chance.
An onion jokes, it makes me cry,
A tomato whispers, 'Give it a try!'

Bees buzzing 'round, in tuxedos they glide,
Pollinating puns with unyielding pride.
The scarecrow chuckles, "What's the buzz here?"
It's just garden humor, bring on the cheer!

Chasing away pests with a rhyme or two,
I realize gardening's quite the zoo.
With laughter as soil, you'll always grow,
And blossom ideas from the roots below.

Verses in Verdant Spaces

In verdant spaces, I trip on the vines,
Reciting my verses, "Oh, how divine!"
They tickle my toes, those green tendrils fair,
Who knew poetry hid in the air?

In the broccoli patch, a sonnet resides,
While carrots recite with their leafy divides.
Each rhubarb's a critic, rolling its eyes,
As I rhyme and stumble amidst all the pies.

The daisies all cheer with their heads held high,
While tulips debate, "Should we laugh or sigh?"
A little frog croaks, "What's your next line?"
"Keep quiet," I snap, "This is my time to shine!"

With humor like sunshine, my verses take flight,
In this garden of laughter, all feels just right.
Each leaf, each stem sings a song quite absurd,
In spaces so verdant, joy's never deterred.

From Roots to Revelations

From roots so deep, new thoughts start to climb,
Digging for wisdom, but hitting a rhyme.
A riddle in soil, a chase through the muck,
Who knew dirty gardening was full of luck?

The basil is wise, dispensing pure sage,
While cilantro jokes in a spicy rampage.
Rosemary chuckles, "What's your secret, my friend?"
I say, "It's just laughter I love to send!"

As I harvest my verses, I tumble and fall,
An onion peeks out, sending tears to us all.
The carrots are snickering, "Just can't you see?
This lesson is simple—don't plant just for me!"

With roots like my thoughts and leaves in the air,
I grow through the laughter, I grow everywhere.
From roots to revelations, I cultivate joy,
As my funny little garden becomes a ploy!

A Garden Symphony

In the garden of sounds, a symphony grows,
With daisies in tune as the music flows.
A trumpet of crickets, a flute of the breeze,
Together they crescendo, nature's reprise.

The tomatoes all hum, while the peppers shake,
To the rhythm of raindrops, a joyful wake.
The seeds argue notes as they sprout and unfold,
Their melodies silly, yet never too bold.

A chicken clucks gently, keeping the beat,
While bunnies hop seemingly light on their feet.
The gardener giggles at this wild affair,
And holds in his hands a pot of fresh air.

As colors collide in a festival grand,
The notes intertwine, a vivacious band.
A garden symphony full of delight,
Where laughter and music fill up the night.

A Tapestry of Blooms

In gardens where the daisies dance,
Bees take a spin, they twist and prance.
The tulips giggle in sunny light,
While daisies plot their floral flight.

With every flap, the butterflies tease,
One lands on a leaf with utmost ease.
Petunias gossip, share their views,
While peas in pods sip morning dews.

The roses smirk with fragrant flair,
They boast of colors, none could compare.
While violets laugh, a playful tease,
As sunflowers lean, swaying in the breeze.

Each bloom a jester, bright and bold,
In gardens wild, their stories told.
Between the rows, a chuckle grows,
In every bud, a punchline shows.

The Ink of Nature

Nature's pen drips hues so bright,
Ink from petals, a joyful sight.
Each drop a giggle, a cheeky wink,
The grass all whispers, 'Come have a drink!'

With every scribble on the breeze,
The wind writes letters through the trees.
Silly squirrels join the grand parade,
Their nutty jokes, a fun charade.

The brook babbles secrets, oh so spry,
In this great book where flowers lie.
Every brushstroke, a story spun,
In this wild script, there's always fun.

Nature's canvas, every shade a laugh,
While clouds above sketch a silly staff.
Each blossom winks, a canvas anew,
In the gallery where humor grew.

Growth in Quiet Corners

In shadowed nooks, the wild things play,
Ferns fold secrets, come what may.
Mossy mats where mushrooms grin,
And beetles march with a silly spin.

The sleepy peas stretch in delight,
While slumbering roots get a good night.
A wayward snail, with swagger carries,
In whispered tones, no one quite buries.

A ladybug dons her red attire,
While hidden critters start a choir.
With every rustle, the laughter rolls,
In secret paths, where humor strolls.

So in corners soft, with flickering light,
Nature blooms with laughter, pure and bright.
Each leaf a jest, each sprout a cheer,
In these quiet spots, joy reappears.

A Symphony of Sprouts

The sprouts assemble, orchestra grand,
Together they play in unity's band.
A squash sings low, a carrot hums,
While radishes beat on their little drums.

The sunflowers stretch, reaching high,
They sway to the melody in the sky.
Each seedling's voice, a note unique,
Together they form a lively peak.

With tickles of wind, the leaves all clap,
As greenery forms its leafy map.
A rhythm of growth, a comical tune,
The veggies groove beneath the moon.

In this garden, laughter takes flight,
As sprouts unite in a joyful night.
Each sprig a note in the earth's own song,
In nature's chorus, we all belong.

Whispers of the Seedbed

In soil so dark, plants start to chat,
With roots that wiggle, like a dance mat.
They gossip of rain, of sun's warm kiss,
As worms join in for a twisty bliss.

The carrots joke, 'We're underground stars!'
While radishes claim they're driving fancy cars.
Oh, peas leap high, sharing wild tales,
Of cabbage kings and lettuce mails.

A sunflower grins, 'I'm the tallest here!'
While a tiny sprout wishes it could appear.
They giggle and chuckle in the warm sun's glow,
As their leafy jokes put on quite the show.

In this wild patch, unwritten dreams sprout,
With friendliest seedlings, no worries, no doubt.
Come join the fun, in this green estate,
Where laughter grows tall, and we all celebrate.

Verses of the Verdant

In vibrant rows, the green crew sings,
Of the joy that each new sprout brings.
With cabbages cracking the silliest jokes,
While daisies dance with invisible folks.

A tomato blushed, 'Am I ripe today?'
While peppers giggle, 'Let's salsa and sway!'
The corn crows loud, 'I'm all ears, you see!'
And the pumpkins roll in sheer jubilee.

The potatoes chuckle underground tight,
'We may be hidden, but we're outta sight!'
The herbs complain of bugs on their leaves,
While their fragrance floats, teasing heartstrings like weaves.

In their green pages, laughter unfolds,
As nature's humor in secret takes hold.
Each verse a delight, in earthy embrace,
In the garden's giggle, we find our place.

Cultivating Dreamscapes

In dreamlike fields where dandelions sprout,
The wishes take flight, let laughter ring out.
A pumpkin and squash are plotting a play,
While the wind joins in, swirling fears away.

The sunflowers shout, 'Here's our big chance!'
With bees buzzing in a furry romance.
They burst into fitful dances alight,
And flutter like confetti in morning's bright.

'What's your flavor?' chimes the mint with a grin,
As thyme chimes in, 'Let the giggles begin!'
With sprigs of parsley, they take to the stage,
In a garden so lively, it's all the rage.

Each moment a verse, in the plots that they weave,
In this joyful place, it's hard to believe.
As seedlings embrace in playful brigade,
This funny patch of earth is lovingly made.

Lines Among the Foliage

Among the green leaves, a secret life thrives,
Where moss meets the rocks as each giggle arrives.
A hedge of hedgehogs overheard in a plight,
'We're on a quest for the leaves that are light!'

The violets whisper, 'A dance we will lead!'
With ants as their partners, they take to the bead.
'We'll twirl, we'll whirl, on a dew-dappled floor,'
As sunlight peeks in, wanting to explore.

In shadows of ferns, a chorus awaits,
Of mushrooms that cheer, holding tiny debates.
'Have you tried the rain?' one shouts with delight,
As others respond, 'It's heavenly, right?'

Each line in the foliage spills colorful cheer,
Where the laughter of nature is always sincere.
So sing with the buds, in this merry parade,
Find joy in the garden where dreams are displayed.

Ink and Ivy

In a garden of ink, where words grow tall,
Pens sprout like flowers, it's fun for all.
With doodles and sketches, they dance in delight,
Chasing butterflies under the moonlight.

Jokes weave through petals, laughter takes flight,
Writing with glee, it feels so right.
Each line a seed, planted with care,
Under the sun, nothing compares.

They twirl in the breeze, these quirky rhymes,
Tickling the funny bone through busy times.
With ink-stained hands, they play and tease,
In this garden of giggles, we do as we please.

So grab your old quill and let it flow,
In the ink and ivy, let creativity glow.
For in every chuckle, a verse will bloom,
In this quirky field, there's always room.

The Cultivator's Quatrain

With shovel in hand, the farmer's on the prowl,
Digging for lines beneath the soil's growl.
Each quatrain planted, a sight to behold,
Sprouting up laughter like marigolds.

He waters with puns, gives weeds a good name,
Every verse that grows is part of the game.
With worms as his friends, they twist and they wring,
In the plot of absurdity, they dance and they sing.

Toolkit of humor, hoe and a spade,
Making the mundane a laughter parade.
Prune back the frown, let sunshine creep in,
In this garden of giggles, we all can win.

So come join the fun, grab a rake if you dare,
Cultivating joy in the open air.
With every quatrain, a smile will sprout,
In this fertile field, laughter's what it's about.

Rhymes that Take Root

Among bedrock of humor, rhymes start to sprout,
They wiggle and jiggle, there's never a doubt.
With giggles that pop like bubbles in the sun,
Each verse is a seed, let's plant and have fun!

In soil rich with puns, we sow what we like,
Wrangling the words, watch them take flight.
Each stanza a sprout, stretching high to the sky,
Hoping for sunshine and laughter nearby.

When clouds roll in, and worries appear,
We tickle the rhymes, make our troubles disappear.
So let's dance in the rain, twirl in the mud,
With verses that giggle, and words that feel good.

In gardens of laughter, we cultivate cheer,
Together we nurture, there's nothing to fear.
For rhymes that take root will always surprise,
With humor to blossom, right before our eyes.

Nature's Lyrical Labyrinth

In a winding maze where giggles abound,
Nature plays tricks, it knows how to clown.
With pathways of verses that twist and that turn,
Every corner a chuckle, there's much to learn.

The trees start to whisper, the bushes they grin,
Each leaf lays a joke, the fun to begin.
With branches a-wobble, they tickle the air,
In this lyrical labyrinth, we've plenty to share.

So follow the path where the oddities grow,
And dance with the daisies in a bright, lively show.
For laughter's the compass when lost in the maze,
In nature's good humor, we'll forever blaze.

Through rhymes and through riddles, the journey is sweet,

With giggles a-plenty, it's never a feat.
So come take a stroll, let joy be your guide,
In this garden of laughter, let your spirit abide.

The Garden of Stanzas

In the garden where poems grow,
Words dance like bees, all aglow.
Each line a flower, bright and neat,
With verses that tickle, oh so sweet.

The gardener laughs at his wild crew,
A rhyme or two sprouting, who knew?
They jostle and wiggle, with flair and style,
Making readers chuckle, mile after mile.

Between the weeds of doubt and rhyme,
Puns tangle up like spaghetti in time.
Planting giggles under the sun,
Watch as the laughter has just begun.

So grab your trowel, let's dig right in,
Where verses sprout, and smiles begin.
In this garden, silliness reigns,
And poetic humor spills like rains.

Rhymes Beneath the Soil

Underneath the earth so deep,
Where funny phrases never sleep.
They wiggle and squirm, waiting to sprout,
With clever puns that shout and pout.

Digging down with a hopeful grin,
Pulling out zany words to spin.
A trowel of joy for every line,
Each little quip, a treasure divine.

Worms wiggle to the comedic beat,
Crawling through verses, oh what a treat!
With giggles hiding in every clump,
Growing tall like a bouncy stump.

So plant a smile, the garden's wide,
With laughter as our trusty guide.
In this patch of joy, we shall toil,
Uncovering rhymes beneath the soil.

Echoes of a Blossoming Heart

In the heart's garden, laughter blooms,
Whimsical echoes, chasing the glooms.
Each beat a joke, a playful jest,
A blossom of joy, it's simply the best.

Puns flutter softly on petal's breeze,
Inviting chuckles with utmost ease.
As words collide in a colorful swirl,
My heart opens wide, letting humor unfurl.

Tickles and giggles arise from the ground,
Where echoes of laughter resound all around.
A bud blooms bright with a cheeky grin,
As the verses chime, let the fun begin!

Here in this garden, the heart feels light,
With every chuckle, the day feels bright.
In the echo of laughter, we find our way,
Through blossoms of joy, come what may.

In the Shadow of Petals

In the shadow of petals, humor hides,
With giggles and quirks, like playful tides.
Sneaky and sly, they peek and play,
Crafting a jest, chasing blues away.

A wink from a daisy, a smirk from a rose,
Petal whispers bring laughter that glows.
Behind leafy shields, quips take their stance,
In this garden of humor, they prance and dance.

Chasing the sunlight, they twirl with glee,
Silly shenanigans, wild and free.
Each shade of color tells a funny tale,
Where blooming chuckles will never pale.

So take a stroll through this whimsical spot,
Where petals echo jokes that hit the dot.
In the shadow they flourish, oh what a sight,
In a world of laughter, everything feels right.

Blooming Thoughts

In gardens bright, where giggles grow,
The daisies dance, the tulips blow.
A clever bee with little charm,
Wears pollen suits, it's quite the arm!

The carrots peek with eyes so round,
They whisper jokes beneath the ground.
While peas all grin and do a jig,
They jest about that leafy twig!

Sunflowers wave with heads held high,
They wink at clouds that float on by.
The tomatoes blush with every glance,
While radishes ponder their next dance!

In this funny patch, no frowns are found,
Just giggles echoing all around.
Each root and stem, in hues so bright,
Chuckle together from day to night.

Nature's Palette

In mixed-up hues, the flowers scheme,
A rainbow riot, it seems a dream.
The yellow daffodils crack jokes,
While purple pansies tease the oaks.

The critters giggle, the rabbits prance,
In this wild world, they take a chance.
A ladybug wears a polka dot,
She's the fashion queen; they love her plot!

The squirrels chatter with acorn caps,
Creating hats and fancy wraps.
While butterflies flirt, the ants march by,
They form a band and sing, oh my!

In nature's art, the fun won't cease,
Each vibrant shade, a little tease.
With laughter blooming across the glade,
In every petal, joy is made!

Harmony in Hedges

The hedges hum a funny song,
As bushes dance all day long.
Each twig aligns in perfect tune,
The grass joins in, beneath the moon!

A hedge of thyme cracks silly puns,
While rosemary slides down for fun.
With laughter sprouting all around,
Four-leaf clovers hop and bound!

The hedgehogs roll in pure delight,
They twirl and twink, a funny sight.
While ivy whispers secrets sweet,
To stately oaks with big, proud feet!

In this green nook, the joy runs wild,
Each leaf and stem, a playful child.
With nature's giggles all aglow,
The world inspires a merry show!

The Fertility of Rhyme

In gardens rife with words so spry,
The verbs play tag, the nouns all fly.
Adjectives stretch to reach the sun,
Each line and verse a playful pun!

The clever rhymes sprout here and there,
They toss their buds into the air.
With laughter looping through each line,
The meter dances, oh so fine!

A stanza folds, a petal curls,
The verses whirl in joyous swirls.
As similes bloom in every hue,
The laughter grows fresh as the dew!

With metaphors sprouting everywhere,
The humor spreads like fragrant air.
In this quirky field of merry chime,
The garden laughs, the fruit is rhyme!

Stanzas in the Soil

In the dirt, I drop my lines,
Hoping for some sunlit signs.
But instead, I get a weed,
Saying, "Dude, you've missed a seed!"

With every chuckle, laughter grows,
My rhymes are spreading like a hose.
The earth can giggle, twist, and dance,
While I just hope for plants to prance.

Fertilizer? I've got a joke,
A pun so good, it made me choke.
Water it well with silly glee,
As this garden laughs along with me.

Compost piles of verse and jest,
In this patch, I try my best.
We'll harvest laughter, weeds, and more,
As stanzas sprout from my garden floor.

Petals of Prose

In blooms of words, I take a spin,
My thoughts take flight, like seeds of whim.
But petals fall on dinner plates,
Who's got the blender? Oh, the fates!

Petal pushers, all in jest,
They huddle close, they know what's best.
With flower crowns of quirky rhymes,
We toast to joy, we toast to chimes.

The nectar's sweet, but oh, beware,
A bee might fly into my hair.
It buzzes loud, can't take a hint,
While I invent a floral stint.

So pluck a line, and watch it fly,
To whirl around, oh my, oh my!
In this bouquet of prose so bright,
We laugh and dance till late at night.

The Garden of Rhyme

In this garden where puns take root,
You might just find a silly fruit.
Grapes that giggle and berries that blush,
All frantically grow in a wordy rush.

A sunflower wears a bowler hat,
While daisies dance with a clever cat.
Be careful where you tread, my friend,
For this patch's humor has no end.

The carrots sing in perfect tune,
While pumpkins chat beneath the moon.
In this patch of verse and rhyme,
We cultivate our joyful time.

So grab a trowel, let's dig in deep,
Where laughter grows and rhymes don't sleep.
With every joke, our garden's fine,
A harvest ripe of mirth divine.

Tending to the Tapestry

Weaving words like vines that climb,
Stitching humor, oh so prime.
A tapestry of funny scenes,
Where laughter's thread unravels dreams.

Colors clash but what a sight,
As giggles tie the knots so tight.
A patchwork quilt of silly grace,
Where every patch brings a smiling face.

From every corner, joy will peek,
And tickle anyone who sneaks.
Unraveling yarns with laughter spun,
A comical dance, oh what a fun!

So tend this tapestry with cheer,
A fabric of fun, come linger near.
In the weave of time, we'll find our way,
Through threads of jest, we laugh and play.

The Soil of Expression

In a garden of giggles, we plant our dreams,
With laughter as water and sunlight in beams.
We sprinkle our puns like seeds in a row,
Hoping to harvest a good laugh or two.

The worms are our partners, they wiggle and dance,
While weeds with their jokes take a mischievous chance.
We dig up our thoughts, they tumble and twirl,
Creating a compost of chuckles and twirls.

Under the surface where humor awaits,
We till through the soil, opening gates.
With each little chuckle, a sprout starts to rise,
In this land of expression, the funny never dies.

So grab a spade and a smile for the ride,
In this plot of absurdity, let's not hide.
For the seeds of our laughter, in rows they will grow,
In the soil of expression, let comedy flow.

Dreams Woven in Green

Amidst leafy laughter, our dreams intertwine,
With vines twisting stories, oh so divine.
Each petal a punchline, each stem a delight,
In this fabric of fun, we'll dance through the night.

We plant our ambitions with snickers and glee,
Hoping for blooms that'll tickle you and me.
The butterflies chuckle, as they flutter about,
In this playful garden, there's never a pout.

Every sprig is a giggle, each bud a surprise,
As we cultivate joy beneath sunny skies.
The fruits of our labor, they shimmer and shine,
In this whimsical world where laughter is fine.

So let's weave our dreams in a tapestry green,
Full of silly stories and scenes yet unseen.
With every chuckle and each grin along the way,
In this garden of mirth, we'll forever play.

Tending to Hidden Treasures

In a patch of delight, we dig down so deep,
Hunting for treasures where giggles can creep.
We dust off our shovels, our joy knows no bounds,
As we find funny nuggets beneath silly mounds.

The weeds hold their secrets, a comical bunch,
They sprout like comedians during our lunch.
With every uprooted laugh, we cheerfully shout,
For the treasures we harvest are what it's about.

Our rakes reveal wonders, in soil enriched,
With stories and puns, our laughter is switched.
Tending to humor, we water with cheer,
Each droplet a chuckle, for all to hear.

So come help us garden, let's get our hands dirty,
In this land of delight, where life is quite flirty.
For in tending our treasures, we flourish with grace,
In the dirt of our dreams, we all find our place.

Flourishing Expressions

In a riot of color, our thoughts start to grow,
With smiles as our sunshine, we put on a show.
Each laugh a petal, brightening the scene,
In this garden of giggles, we reign as the queen.

We water our stories with humor so pure,
In rows of delight, where the punchlines endure.
The bees buzz in harmony, pollinating cheer,
Multiplying joy with every zany idea.

As we trim back the worries, prune off the frowns,
We'll scatter our laughter like confetti in towns.
With fragrant expressions, so bold and so bright,
In the blooming of nonsense, we revel in light.

So join in this frolic, let's flourish and play,
In this wild garden where whimsy holds sway.
With every giggle, our harvest comes round,
In this field of expressions, pure joy can be found.

Threads of Life

In gardens green, the gnomes do dance,
With watering cans, they take their chance.
They sprinkle seeds of dreams and jest,
While rabbits plot their carrot quest.

Each flower blooms, a quirky sight,
Waving to bees in pure delight.
The sun with shades, oh what a show,
While ants hold meetings down below.

Breaking Ground

Let's dig a hole, and find some fun,
Who knew that dirt could weigh a ton?
A shovel slips, and down I go,
As worms all giggle, stealing the show.

The soil's rich with laughter sweet,
In every clump, a tasty treat.
We plant our hopes with silly gloves,
And sing to plants that play like loves.

Metaphors in Bloom

A daisy sprouted with a grin,
It said, "My friend, let summer in!"
The tulips twirled in fancy hats,
While daisies giggled at the fats.

In every bud, a tale to tell,
Of sunshine, rain, and playful swell.
With puns like petals in the breeze,
We dance with joy, oh yes, with ease!

The Fertile Imagination

In plots of dreams where veggies grow,
A pumpkin sculptor steals the show.
With witty harvests and funny seeds,
The world's a garden of wild creeds.

Turnip turnarounds, what a sight!
A cabbage queen, full of delight.
With every sprout, the laughter flows,
In every row, a story grows.

Echoes in the Earth

Digging down with a trowel,
I found a sock and a vowel.
Worms are laughing, having a ball,
While daisies rock, singing, "Y'all!"

Under a moonbeam's bubble,
I plant my thoughts, causing trouble.
Potatoes grin at my mischief,
"Trowel, come here, let's make a riff!"

Roots tickle and dance around,
As I juggle seeds on the ground.
Laughter twinkles in the dirt,
All while the radishes flirt!

The garden's a stage, all aglow,
With carrots that steal every show.
Watch out for peas with a quip,
They'll make you laugh till you trip!

Flourishing in Stanza

In a plot where the verses grow,
Each rhyme sprouted in a row.
A sunflower winks, says, "Hello,"
While poets giggle at the show.

Beans entwined in a playful twist,
Composed a sonnet, couldn't resist.
Tomatoes burst with juicy glee,
Correlating their growth to me!

A pun-filled weeding with glee,
Pulling thyme with some melody.
Each stanza grows its own bright tune,
Harvesting giggles beneath the moon.

Nature's eager to take the stage,
In plots of rhyme, we turn the page.
With every sentence planted just right,
The garden fills with pure delight!

The Harvest of Hope

In baskets of laughter, we collect,
All the puns that we can select.
Turnips wave with a cheeky grin,
While zucchinis giggle, letting us in.

We celebrate the crops with glee,
As chard sings out, "Here's a spree!"
Radishes cheer in a funky dance,
While peppers join in, taking a chance.

With each rooted joke that we sow,
The harvest grows, putting on a show.
A field of smiles scattered 'round,
Laughter echoes, a joyful sound!

So gather your thoughts, let them sprout,
Life's full of humor, without a doubt.
With every seed of joy we cast,
The harvest of hope is unsurpassed!

Rhythms in the Rain

As raindrops dance on the soil's floor,
Each droplet makes the garden roar.
The carrots tap their tiny toes,
While tomatoes sway, wearing their clothes.

Worms in puddles, doing a jig,
With cabbage heads, they all dig.
A rinse, a roll, a splash, a cheer,
With beats that make the plants draw near.

Clouds perform a rhythm divine,
While peppers and beans sip on wine.
They talk in rhymes, with beats so sweet,
As every veggie moves to the beat.

So let the rain sing us a tune,
With each raindrop's rhythm, life's a boon.
In this garden, let laughter reign,
We're grooving along to nature's refrain!

Seeds of Thought

In the garden of my mind, I plant,
A kernel of an idea, oh what a slant.
Some sprout up with leaves, so grand and green,
While others just sit there, looking mean.

I water them with laughter, make them grow,
But some just giggle and refuse to show.
The weeding of the doubts, a constant chore,
Pulling roots of worry from the floor.

Every now and then, a flower blooms,
With petals so bright, banishing glooms.
I dance around my thoughts, a silly sight,
Chasing the weeds that try to take flight.

So if you see my garden, don't be shy,
Join me in this folly, we'll reach the sky.
Together we'll plant seeds, let them sprout,
In this jolly patch, there's never a drought.

Lines That Take Root

Lines that wiggle and twist in the ground,
With a giggle, they leap, oh what a sound!
Each stanza a sprout, with rhymes as its leaves,
In this plot of nonsense, everyone believes.

I dig in the dirt with a trowel of cheer,
As verses come dancing, don't disappear.
Some silliness grows, while some seem to flop,
But who cares if it's funny? We'll never stop!

I plant them in clusters, in rows all askew,
Where humor and puns sprout like morning dew.
The roots intertwine in a tangled ball,
In this garden of giggles, we'll have a ball!

So come, grab a shovel, let's plant something neat,
With laughter as sunlight, our harvests are sweet.
Lines take root where joy freely flows,
In this wacky garden, there's space for all those!

The Harvest of Dreams

In the field of my thoughts, where the funny grows,
Dreams ripen and tumble like wind-blown rows.
I wait for the harvest with a grin on my face,
While giggles and chuckles fill up every space.

The sweetness of laughter, a bountiful yield,
As I gather my dreams from this chaotic field.
Some dreams are a mess, all tangled and wild,
But others shine brightly, like a joyous child.

With baskets of puns and jokes in the sun,
I wish for a festival of laughter and fun.
The silly and sweet in this harvest we share,
Dancing with giggles, floating in the air.

So let's gather 'round and sing silly songs,
As we feast on our dreams, where each laughter belongs.
In this quirky cornucopia, joy spills out wide,
Harvesting smiles as the silly dreams glide.

Luminescent Blooms

Under the moonlight, where giggles ignite,
Blooms of bright humor gleam in the night.
With petals of laughter, so vibrant and free,
Each flower's a punchline, come giggle with me!

I chase after shadows, where silliness hides,
These luminous dreams are my fanciful guides.
Some bloom into madness, while others take flight,
Dancing on breezes, such a comical sight.

The garden of humor, all colors and fun,
With seeds of delight, under the warm sun.
I gather the petals, each giggle a spark,
These luminescent blooms light up the dark.

So wander with me through this festival bright,
Where laughter takes root every day and night.
Together we'll revel in this floral parade,
In a world full of whimsy, we're never dismayed.

Roots of Reflection

In a patch of dirt, I toss my dreams,
With a shovel and a grin, or so it seems.
The vegetables chuckle, as they take their stand,
While the weeds plot mischief, like a sneaky band.

I planted my thoughts, but they tangled up tight,
Carrots confused with wisecracks in flight.
Tomatoes are rolling, laughing out loud,
While radishes whisper, 'We're exceptionally proud!'

Sunshine beams down, sharing silly jokes,
As dancing daisies prance, oh what folk!
I'll harvest the laughter that I've sown here,
With roots of reflection, it's perfectly clear.

So here in the garden, where humor does bloom,
I encourage each seed to escape from its gloom.
And perhaps shed a tear—of laughter, not pain,
For the roots hold the stories, time and again.

Arcadia's Ascent

In a world where bushes wear hats and shoes,
I climbed old trees, just to shake off my blues.
A snail with a scroll, wrote whimsical lore,
While a squirrel turned bard, singing songs galore.

The bees buzzed in rhythm, with a witty sting,
They'd argue about flowers—who'd win the bling.
A frog croaked an aria, off key and loud,
And the daisies erupted, cheering it proud.

With every tall climb on my quest for delight,
The branches would creak, but it felt just right.
I'd chat with the clouds as they shaped silly forms,
Sending giggles to earth in the midst of the storms.

In Arcadia's ascent, I found joy and jest,
Amid whispering leaves, a comedic fest.
Who knew that in nature, the prize goes untold—
In laughter and light, the heart can be bold!

The Poetic Gardener

They say I'm a poet, with a green thumb too,
But my plants think my rhymes are just a bad brew.
"I'd rather you hum, than recite such a strain!"
Said a cantankerous cabbage, in leaf a bit vain.

The carrots rolled eyes, in their tucked little rows,
As I chanted for sun on gray mornings, with woes.
'Your verse isn't fertile!' the radishes hissed,
While dandelions giggled, in humorous bliss.

But who knew a seed could hold so much flair?
As I spun tales of thunder from out of thin air.
The sprouts began dancing, a whimsical show,
While the lettuce just sighed, 'Why can't we all grow?'

So I garden in laughter, with rhymes in my pot,
To coax all the blooms from their humorless spot.
In this patch of wit, where the fun never wanes,
I'll be the poetic gardener—sowing joy in my veins.

Threads of Nature's Narrative

In the loom of the earth, I weave my delight,
With threads made of laughter and colors so bright.
Ladybugs dance, doing pirouettes grand,
While a butterfly quips, 'Watch my wings, isn't it planned?'

The sun takes a bow, in a glow of pure fun,
As shadows play games, on the ground they have spun.
While worms in the dirt write comedic tales,
Of ants with their groceries and wind in their sails.

Trees gossip above, while roots intertwine,
Whispering secrets of the grapevines divine.
"I'm tired of rain, let's flirt with the clouds,"
Murmured a passel of petals, all giggling loud.

Threads of nature's tale, woven fine in the breeze,
Shows that humor's a harvest, that grows with such ease.
With every crisp laugh, let's nurture the earth,
For the funniest threads give the truest rebirth.

Growth of the Muse

In a garden where words collide,
The rhymes come out to play and hide.
Catch a verb as it leaps high,
And let metaphors fill the sky.

With puns that sprout beneath my feet,
I laugh at rhymes both short and sweet.
A stanza stirs like a rumbling beast,
As the similes host a fanciful feast.

The vector of thoughts begins to twist,
While I ponder, then clench my fist.
In this plot of prose, oh what delight,
As tomatoes tell stories far into the night.

So when inspiration comes to tease,
I'll dance with joy around these trees.
For every line that wiggles and hops,
There's a delightful harvest that never stops.

Blossoms Beneath the Moon

Under the glow of lunar beams,
Words awaken from their dreams.
Dancing flowers in verse and prose,
Giggle in whispers, the night knows.

The daisies chuckle with cheeky flair,
While the tulips swap tales without care.
A daffodil trips on a naughty pun,
And laughter erupts as if on the run.

The moon laughs softly, a watchful eye,
At verses that tumble and sometimes fly.
Starlight twinkles with a witty grin,
As the humor blooms, embracing the skin.

A garden of giggles in every nook,
Growing bright letters, like a happy book.
Blooming bright laughter in every line,
In this nighttime chorus, all's divine.

Bounty of the Bard

In fields of verse, where jesters roam,
The Bard has made this place his home.
With quips and quotes that twist and turn,
Making every soul laugh and yearn.

Barley sings while oats do jig,
As the cozy rhymes decide to dig.
Lettuce leaves laugh at all the fuss,
While carrots whisper, "Join us, just!"

A banquet spread 'neath the trees so tall,
Where every rhyme takes a goofy fall.
The harvest yields a bounteous cheer,
For words sown well will bring good beer.

So come, dear friend, let's share the fun,
As the bounty of laughter keeps us spun.
With each quirk and giggle, we'll make it last,
In the fields where the Bard's bright humor's cast.

Clairvoyance Among the Crops

I peep through rows of bushel suns,
Where corn whispers secrets, having fun.
The vegetables chat in a knowing spree,
While herbs craft futures, with glee in thee.

Oh, the carrots argue with the peas,
On the best way to tease the breeze.
Tomatoes declare they can predict,
How many puns will be inflict.

And as the lettuce starts to dance,
I wonder if fate gives them a chance.
For every stalk that bends in laughter,
The harvest seems to chase after.

Clairvoyant green in this leafy spree,
The laughter echoes, enlivened and free.
In the garden of wit, we shall creep,
Where humor's harvest grows ever deep.

Cultivating Dreams

In the garden of my mind, I plant,
Dreams like seeds, popping up with a chant.
Water them with laughter, sun-filled rays,
Watch them grow in the silliest ways.

Strawberries wear hats, carrots dance,
Radishes twirl, given half a chance.
With butterflies juggling, bees sing tunes,
In this patch of whimsy under the moons.

Tending my thoughts with a playful hand,
Weeds of worry cannot withstand.
For each silly thought is a flower bright,
Blooming in joy, oh what a sight!

So, let's chuckle together in this plot,
Sow the seeds of mirth, forget what's hot.
With giggles as fertilizer, let's cheer,
Life's a garden - plant love every year!

Nature's Lullabies

Crickets croon under the silver spree,
While frogs jump high in harmony.
Fireflies flash like notes in the night,
Nature's chorus keeps spirits light.

Trees whisper secrets the wind can't confine,
With a tickle of branches, it's all so fine.
The moon chuckles, casting shadows so sweet,
As pixies tap dance along the beat.

Roses gossip, petals aflutter,
While daisies giggle, what a clutter!
And in this garden of crazy delight,
Even the stones hum songs of the night.

So let's sway together, hand in hand,
Join the laughter in this merry land.
With the soil of humor, let's sprout some cheer,
In nature's embrace, there's naught to fear!

Phrases Amongst the Foliage

Words scatter like seeds upon the trail,
Dancing with breezes, none to fail.
Puns grow as ivy, climbing up high,
In this leafy corner where witticisms lie.

Leaves gossip softly under a cloud,
And rattling branches speak out loud.
Each phrase a sprout, with roots entrenched,
In the humor and laughter we all quench.

Vines twist and turn, weaving their tales,
With laughter as rain, this garden prevails.
Words tickle like petals in the softest breeze,
Writing my sonnets with the greatest of ease.

So pluck a line, and plant it near,
Let it flourish with chuckles, let's cheer!
Amongst the foliage, let's keep it real,
For every phrase sown is a joke we feel!

Pruning Prose

With snips and cuts, I tend my lines,
Shearing away the dull, finding shines.
Thorns of boredom tossed in the bin,
Creating a garden where giggles begin.

A little trim here, a snip there too,
Chasing away the critic's view.
Each word pruned, with laughter in bloom,
Filling this space, it's fun's little room.

Clippings of worries, compost with glee,
Turning old phrases into spree.
With every snip, the jests take flight,
A crazed bouquet of delight in sight.

So join me now in this gardening quest,
Where writing's a pleasure, a silly fest.
With pruning shears, let's weed the prose,
To uncover the laughs, and happiness grows!

Where Words Take Flight

In the garden of phrases, we plant our dreams,
Among giggles and chuckles, it's not as it seems.
Words sprout like daisies, so bright and so bold,
Stories unfurl in the sunlight, uncontrolled.

With a wink and a grin, the puns take their stand,
Each syllable bounces, a playful band.
The verses take flight on the wings of a jest,
In the laughter of lines, we find our quest.

Rhymes dance like bunnies, in crazy ballet,
Twisting and turning in a witty display.
With each little rhyme, comes a tickle, a tease,
In gardens of humor, we plant with ease.

So let our words blossom, let joy come alive,
In the soil of laughter, our verses will thrive.
For every good pun needs a season to shine,
In the playground of poetry, we'll don our best line.

Nurturing Artistry

In a patch where creativity sprouts every day,
We water our dreams in an idle ballet.
With pots full of giggles and sunshine in hand,
We nurture, we tickle, we doodle, we stand.

Painting with words on the canvas of light,
Our brushes are silly, painting wrongs into right.
Each stroke is a chuckle, each hue a delight,
In the gallery of laughter, our spirits take flight.

Oh, the art of the pun, it's a delicate craft,
With lines that are funny, the world can't help but laugh.
We sketch with our hearts, leaving echoes of cheer,
In the nursery of laughter, we hold our dreams dear.

So gather, dear friends, in this garden of mirth,
Let's plant little verses that spring from the earth.
With quirky creations and whimsical flair,
We'll nurture our artistry with joy in the air.

From Bud to Bloom

From a bud of a thought, we water our laughs,
Each petal a line, in our playful epitaphs.
With sunshine of smiles, and rain of delight,
We wait for the blossoms to burst into sight.

The quirky creations, with colors so bright,
Unfold in the warmth of a glorious night.
Each phrase is a blossom, in gardens we roam,
We laugh at our verses, they feel like home.

As the humor all grows in the back of our minds,
We've fashioned a plot with the quirkiest finds.
From blooms that are silly to sprouts of pure glee,
Our garden of laughter, come wander with me.

With each giggle and snort, our seedlings will sway,
In the breeze of the banter, they dance and they play.
From bud to a bloom, let's cherish our craft,
In the fields of our humor, let's wander and laugh.

The Dance of the Leaves

Leaves rustle in laughter, a whimsical waltz,
Skittish and funny, no need for a pulse.
With each little whisper, they twirl in delight,
A giggle of breezes, a dance in the night.

From tiptoeing tendrils to swirling in air,
The leaves share their secrets with such flair.
They sway with the rhythm, they twist and they shout,
Each leaf tells a story, there's never a doubt.

With a chuckle or two, they shimmy and glide,
In the forest of puns, they'll never hide.
They tumble and tumble in zany loops,
In this hilarious fest, they form merry groups.

So join in the fun, take a leaf from their book,
In the dance of the leaves, just take a good look.
For in every twirl, in every cheeky tease,
There's joy in the movement, a laugh in the breeze.

www.ingramcontent.com/pod-product-compliance
Lightning Source LLC
Chambersburg PA
CBHW071845160426
43209CB00003B/416